Foot Passenger Europe

Travel Europe for less without driving or flying

Richard Penn

Many thanks to Dave and Jane Penn for their diligent checking and excellent advice. All remaining errors are my own.

Airbnb is a registered trademark of Airbnb, Inc., 888 Brannan Street, 4th Floor, San Francisco, CA 94103, United States. Airbnb does not endorse the content of this book, is not responsible for its content, and has not sponsored the writing of it. All trademarks are used without endorsement or sponsorship.

The ideas in this book are based on my own personal experience and should not be construed as professional advice. The author is not responsible for any consequences of following these ideas.

For updates and addenda, see the webpage footPassenger.org, the Facebook page @footPassenger or contact me at dickpenn@gmail.com.

Purchasers of the e-book or paperback versions of this 2019 edition may obtain the 2020 e-book at no charge, when it becomes available. Follow the Foot Passenger Europe Facebook page for news.

Dewey™ Library Classification: 914.045

Contents

1 Introduction

This small book is for the modern adventure traveller – not the adrenaline junkie who leaps off tall buildings, but one who wants to see historic and scenic places as cheaply as possible, to have some contact with the people in those places, and to have the sense of travelling in the landscape rather than travelling over it.

Split, Croatia

New booking services like Airbnb have joined traditional rail and coach travel to make this a richer and easier way to travel, and to save us all money. I generally budget £1200 for a four-week trip from the UK, and see four to six cities across Europe.

Genoa Central Station

If you need someone with an umbrella to lead you everywhere, this is not for you. To be clear, foot-passenger

travel is not the easiest or the cheapest way to get anywhere. Budget airlines provide that, and they work really well. Maybe I'm old-fashioned, but to me, this feels more like real travel. You need plenty of time, and you need to accept that delay is part of the process.

2 Trip planning

Where to go

This is my purely subjective map of where it seems safe to travel. I've completely ruled out Russia and its affiliated states, most of the Arab world, Serbia, Kosovo and North Macedonia. I'd look carefully at Morocco, Algeria, most of Turkey, and Jordan. Having visited Israel, Bosnia-Herzegovina and North Cyprus, I experienced no problems, but there is a distinct air of tension in those places, and you have to be careful. I'd expect Ukraine to be similar, but of course stay away from the conflict zones in Crimea and the Donbass.

The authoritative source for all these decisions is the Foreign Office travel advice site; they provide details about where to go and what to avoid. It can be a bit conservative at times. For example, they recommend avoiding all buses in Israel because of the risk of bombs, which aren't really all that common. But read very carefully if you are planning to visit the West Bank in any way except a guided tour or a tourist taxi.

If you are a woman travelling alone, openly gay or transgender, you need to take heed of specific advice on the site; some people in Arab countries in particular have pretty medieval attitudes. I think it's also worth mentioning the fact when booking Airbnb places. Of course, you have the right to equal treatment, but attitudes out there are not everything we would like them to be, and it's better to be turned down during the booking process than turned away at the door.

I tend to travel to poorer places, ones that are off the main tourist routes. One reason is that they're cheaper; everything in the shops is less expensive, and rooms can be much more economical. You can rent a flat for a week in a place like Sarajevo or Corsica for the price of a single night in London or Zurich. That means more travel for your money. Travel is also cheap: €15 buys you a 6-hour coach journey in much of Eastern Europe.

These places are often more interesting than the west. Countries that have struggled to drag themselves into mainstream Europe after decades of oppression, fishing villages that still operate inshore with small boats, cities that have barely changed since the 1950's, or even the 1590's. Sometimes, western culture seems like a steamroller, flattening and homogenising people's lives until we all live the same way. That's the "beaten track," and I enjoy being off it.

Train, coach or air

Broadly speaking, the train is faster in western Europe, and coaches are faster in former eastern-bloc countries. There are exceptions, and you will need to research specific journeys.

The railway stations in some former communist countries are run down and abandoned, while coach companies vie for your business outside.

Split, Croatia (both pictures)

Google Maps is generally reliable in the West, but some coach companies don't appear, so Google may tell you to use the train when it isn't the best option. A web-page search for "(city) to (city) bus" will often turn up lines the map applications don't include. Also, try the excellent Bus Radar website. If you're already out there, go to the central coach station and look at the posters or ask at the office. The coach station ("inter-city bus") is not always the same as the central station for city buses, and again, the map applications don't understand the difference.

Coaches ("Autobus" in most languages, *Ow-toh-boose*, not *Awe-toe-bus*) are generally comfortable and reliable in rich and middling countries, but can be an adventure in poor ones – in North Cyprus for example, it feels like going back fifty years, each minibus having two burly guards alongside the driver.

Lefkosa (North Nicosia)

Flying

I am a reluctant user of aeroplanes. Apart from the environmental issues, they cut you off from the people and places you fly over. You also spend hours in airports, some of the nastiest buildings ever devised. They are often hard to get to, negating much of the benefit of faster travel. I must confess an emotional attachment to trains and ferries – for me, that is real travel. However, I typically do book a return flight on long journeys, as multi-day travel seems less appealing when going back home.

Points to watch when planning air travel:

- The cheapest flights generally leave very early in the morning or arrive late at night. Factor in the cost of a hotel near the airport or a long taxi ride, and consider paying a little more.
- Low-cost airlines are expert at adding on charges. You may pay an extra €30 to check a bag, and the one you are allowed to carry on board may be tiny. You may pay to reserve a seat, or end up in a scramble for the middle seats nobody wants. National carriers like SAS or Alitalia are often reasonable when you add up all the charges, and are more likely to fly at reasonable times.
- Think about the cost of travel from the airport in the UK. If, like me, you live in a part of England with dreadful

trains, you may have to stay overnight near the airport: another added cost.

- UK residents need to allow extra time on check-in; there's a special, slow line for non-Schengen passengers, and that's going to be even slower if Brexit happens. Or you can go fast-track for yet another extra charge.
- Don't restrict yourself to airports right at your destination. Many cheap flights go to obscure airports, but a train can get you to the city in an hour or so.

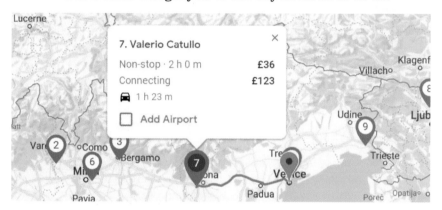

Google™© Flights, "nearby airports" feature

Ferries

I must confess to an irrational love of ferries. To me, they are the epitome of travel. On the other hand, ferry travel has some gotchas, as well:

- For journeys of more than a couple of hours, they usually travel overnight. Unless you like to sleep sitting up, that means an extra charge for a cabin. In season, about €60, out of season €40. This is a particular issue for single travellers, as most cabins have two or four beds and it's less economical if you are alone. Some companies that put strangers together in shared cabins; this is very rare, but check with the operating company.
- Not all ferries run daily. Trip planning is more complex with ships that only sail once or twice a week.

Times of the year

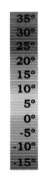

As a retired person, I can travel whenever I want, so I tend to travel out of season. It's cheaper, trains have plenty of seats, and people have more time to help you. Of course, the downside is the weather.

Here is the average temperature chart[1] for January. For me, an average in the 10- to 20-degree range is comfortable, so I'd be looking somewhere around the Mediterranean or in Spain.

As I write, I'm in Sicily in February, and it's quite comfortable. Note: green on these maps is not good, it's cold.

---

1 These images are CC-BY openstreetmap.org, used under Open Data licence from mappedplanet.com and may be copied or distributed only under similar terms.

In April or October, virtually all of Europe is in a
comfortable range. Only northern Scandinavia, Iceland and
the Alps are colder, and many would find it OK, even
there.

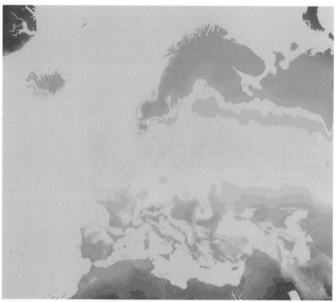

In July, the situation is reversed. The Alps and everything to the north are comfortable, while southern Spain, Africa and the Middle East are way too hot. If you're a beach person, anywhere on the Med will be fine, but you won't want to wear much, city tours will be more gruelling, and everything is crowded.

The best thing to do in August is to stay home or visit somewhere in the UK. Everything is crowded and expensive, and none of the local people are in their own cities, especially in France. For much more data on this, including rainfall and sunny-day averages, see the Wikipedia article Climate of Europe.

Some other considerations: many attractions are seasonal, like Oktoberfest and the Christmas markets in Germany. There are times to be avoided, like Ramadan in Muslim countries, when many attractions will be closed. Whole sections of old Jerusalem are closed off. Ramadan presently falls in late spring, but it moves from year to year. For details, see Ramadan in Wikipedia.

Days of the week

Many museums are closed on Monday, so it's a good day for travel. Big stores open on Sunday, but local markets and small shops close. Churches and cathedrals may restrict visitors on Sundays. These are the patterns in most Christian countries, but check city tourism websites or the tourist office, as local customs may differ. On busy routes, Saturday is a good travel day, as you don't have to battle commuters. Trains may be scarce or start later on Sunday. Tickets may also be cheaper on weekends.

Don't assume Airbnb stays have to be Saturday to Saturday, though this is a common convention for cottage rentals. People seem to be OK with any days. Some hosts may prefer a later check-in on weekdays, 1800 or later, because they work during the week.

Israel is a special case. Saturday is the day when everything shuts down, and it is observed much more strictly than in Europe, so don't plan to arrive or leave on that day. Trams and buses may not run, and only Arab taxis operate, so they are in short supply. Additional holy days, usually Sundays, are observed even more strictly, with few people even driving their own cars.

How long to travel

This may depend on what else you have to do, but I like a long trip, at least three weeks, preferably four. On a long trip, if something goes wrong with your arrangements, you can just take a day off. Go to the town square, have a beer. On a short trip, every delay can feel like a disaster.

For trips of more than four weeks, there are a few housekeeping items you need to check. If you own your home, check whether the insurance company needs to be notified. Usually, that's for trips of more than 31 days. If you rent, you may need to notify your landlord, for the same reason. If you have annual travel insurance, check the limit on the length of trips. If you exceed that limit (also usually 31 days, but Saga™ does 45 days) you may need expensive single-trip insurance. Get somebody to pick up your mail while you're away, and check the house for broken windows and the like.

How long to stay

Personally, I like to stay at least three nights in any given place. I will occasionally stay a single night if I'm there for an early flight or ferry sailing, but I don't like to go somewhere and not see it. Three nights means two full days; one to soak up the atmosphere and find out what's to see, and the second to do the actual sightseeing and take photos.

Larger places, of course, justify longer stays. I generally don't stay more than a week, and that may include one day of doing almost nothing. But a big city like Paris or Berlin can provide as many days of fascinating sights as you can stand before the wanderlust kicks in.

It's a bit more economical to stay more days. Most Airbnb places have a 10% discount for seven nights, and there's often a cleaning charge or booking charge up to €30 per stay. Remember to specify the length of your stay before you start searching, as some places don't appear in results if you're only staying one or two nights.

Conversely, I wouldn't stay in one room more than a week. To see a particular city for more than that, book the first week at Airbnb and leave the remaining days unplanned. You may find somewhere else you like in the area, or you may find a nearby town with new attractions.

Not all Airbnb

I am talking here about the low-cost end of the Airbnb market. They cover a broad range, including some real luxury places, but it is the low end where they are unique. You can book fancy villas through travel agents or other sites, but Airbnb is really the only option for renting ordinary flats and rooms from ordinary people.

Don't over-plan

Travel planning is fun, and the web services make it easy. It's like fantasy travel. But if you book every aspect of your

trip in advance, you become a slave to that schedule. If
you're enjoying a place, your plan may drag you away. If a
ferry is delayed or you miss a connection, it's a disaster as
all your onward journeys go without you. Travel out of
season, and there is no need for all that. Every train, and
particularly every ferry, will be half-empty, and there are
always rooms available. Here's the queue at the main
station in Palermo, in February.

I generally book my escape from the UK in detail, and have
a return trip (usually a flight) booked ahead of time.
Otherwise, I go from day to day, booking accommodation a
few days ahead. However, if you travel anywhere that
requires a visa, check their requirements, as it may be
mandatory to have an onward or return ticket out of that
country.

3 Crossing the channel

That hole

Photo credit: Florian Fèvre from Mobilys

Let's get this out of the way first: yes, I know there's a tunnel under the channel, and indeed it is the fastest and most convenient way to get to the continent.

My choice to smell the sea and see foreign parts appearing gradually out of a misty horizon is purely personal. If you want to make the trip in a steel box in a hole in the ground, go for it. See the Eurostar™ website for more not Eurotunnel™, which is for car drivers.

Channel ferries

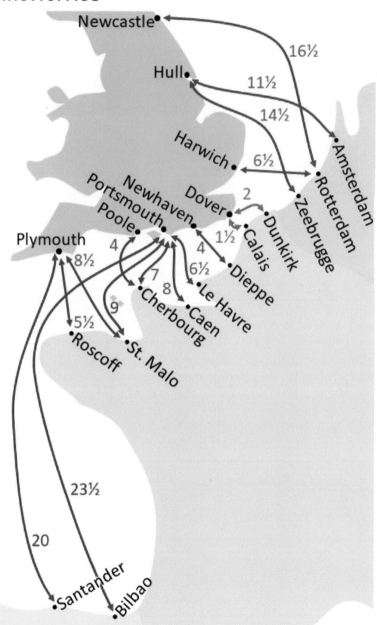

Short-distance ferries running during the day are the most economical. For an overnight ferry, you'll pay at least £40 to include a cabin, unless you can sleep in a chair. Many daytime ferries either leave early or arrive late, so you'll need to book a night in or near the ferry port; seldom the most attractive place to stay. See *Ferry Timetables* on page 73 for details, as your best choice will depend on where you live, as well as where you're headed. If you live a long way from Dover, some of the longer routes might be better. Weigh up the overall cost, including rail or coach fares and any overnight stays in the ferry ports. The timetables in this book are approximate, so do more research on sites such as Direct Ferries, Bus Radar and the operating companies.

Ferry times need to be taken with a large dose of reality. Modern ports cater to cars and lorries, considering the humble foot passenger to be an anachronism. Ferry companies advise foot passengers to arrive at least an hour before they sail (90 minutes for some), and transfers to and from the nearest station may require long walks on obscure and forgotten paths, or a taxi ride that will add to your expense. Only two channel ports are close to a mainline station on the English side: Newhaven and Harwich. On the continental side, only Roscoff, Dieppe and Le Havre are near their stations. In Calais, the main-line station (Calais-Fréthun) is ten miles from the ferry port, via a two-mile walk and a train ride. Allow at least two hours at each end for the Dover routes. At Hoek van Holland, for Rotterdam, a private coach needs to be pre-booked with the ferry ticket, again adding time and cost.

Being a foot passenger on a ferry is perhaps a thing of the past, and the companies seem determined to drive us away, but I persist with it just because I enjoy it. Crossing the channel any other way just isn't proper travel.

Here's that chart again, but with more realistic journey times, to get from main station to main station, and to allow arrival an hour before sailing.

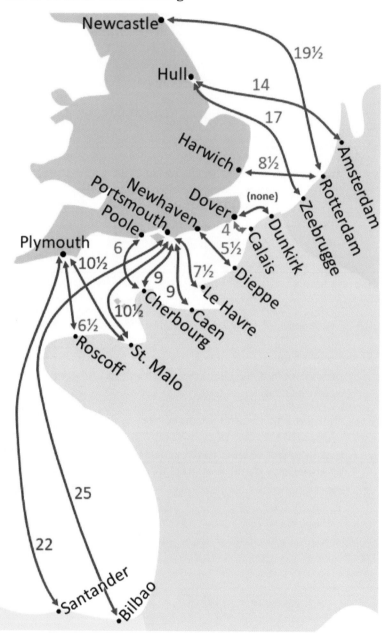

4 Travel maps

In this section, I include a number of timing maps, for travel across Europe. You can get more general ones from railway and bus companies, but here I focus specifically on travel from Britain. Be careful in interpreting them; you can't just add up a number of links to get a journey time. There will always be a wait for your next train, and transfers can take some time, especially in cities without a main station. For rail travel, trust the Rail Europe site, or any of the national rail companies (except the British one, which doesn't know about Europe).

Google Maps can also give you an exact route and timing, but don't rely on it for ferry times. It doesn't know how ferries join up with trains, because it assumes that they're for cars and lorries. For Calais, use Calais-Fréthun as your starting point, but allow two hours for your slog from the ferry port. For the Netherlands ports, remember that the foot-passenger bus will take you to Rotterdam or Amsterdam; you can't start from the port.

Netherlands and Germany

This chart covers Germany, and will also be your first step if you are travelling towards Poland, Czechia or Scandinavia.

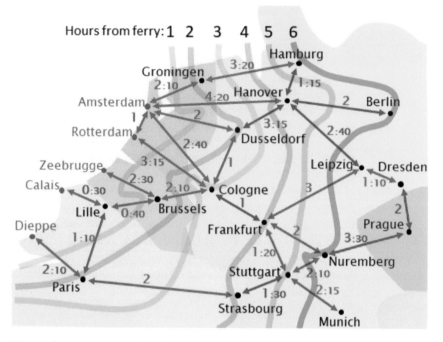

Here, the east coast ferries may give you an advantage. Because the ferry ride is overnight, you have a whole day to travel, so any of these places is within a reasonable day's journey.

If you're starting in the south or west of England, or heading for southern Germany, the Calais or Dieppe options still look better. There's no point to travelling north in England just to get a ferry to carry you south. For more detail, see *Ferry Timetables* on page 73.

If you are heading for eastern Europe, try a stay in Berlin, Dresden or Munich. Stay a few days, there's a lot to see. From there, consider coaches as well as trains.

France, Spain and Morocco

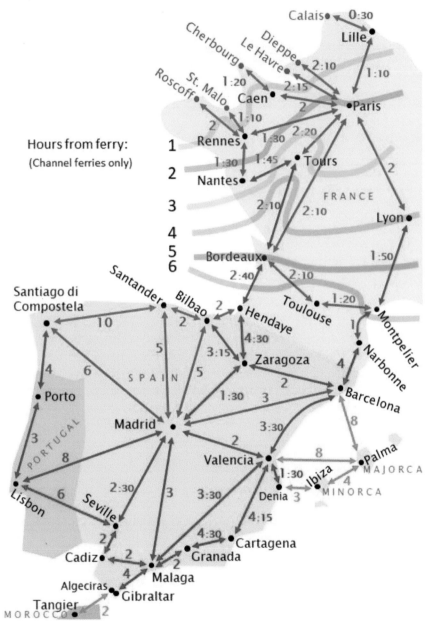

The easiest way to get to anywhere in Spain is to take one of the <u>Brittany Ferries</u> ships, from Portsmouth or Plymouth to Santander or Bilbao. They aren't cheap, but they cut out a

lot of travel in France. As I write this, a Plymouth to
Santander sailing in May is £184. It's only £99 if you book
an "airline seat" instead of a cabin, and cabin costs are
shared if you're not alone. The airline seats are actually
pretty good; better than anything you'll find on an
aeroplane.

As far as channel ferries go, you might expect that more
westerly ferries from England would save some journey time
for Spain. This might be true if you are driving a car, but
not for train travellers. Because the SNCF network is so
Paris-centred, the quickest journeys always involve
changing there, so Dieppe or Calais is faster than anywhere
else. If you aim to travel slowly and enjoy places along the
way, Roscoff or St. Malo is still a reasonable option,
especially if you live in the west of England. For example,
Portsmouth to St. Malo is only £99 including a cabin,
getting you there early in the morning.

If you are changing in Paris, bear in mind that, like London,
it doesn't have a central station. You'll be schlepping your
bags up and down Metro escalators, and you need to allow
adequate time for that. The *Gare du Nord* is a short walk to
the *Gare de L'Est,* and *Austerlitz* is attached to *Gare de
Lyon*, but all the other combinations involve Metro travel.
The SNCF booking website allows a lot of time for crossing
the city, so you may do better to reserve only your ticket to
Paris, and book the second leg from your departure station.

Local train in Cartagena, by [Øyvind Holmstad](#) on Wikimedia

The train in Spain is mostly a bit of a pain. Away from the
Riviera or Madrid, they're not fast and not cheap. For
example, Bordeaux to Valencia is £94 and takes over 10
hours. Look at [Bus Radar](#) for alternatives.

It's also worth noting that your best route to Barcelona or the Riviera is via Lyon and the south coast of France. An example of this is Dieppe to Barcelona: nearly eleven hours, and £110; more than I would like to do in one day. I would plan a night or two in Lyon or Narbonne, if I were taking that route.

Narbonne

The bottom line is that you should take the train through France only if you like taking trains through France. They are lovely trains, to be honest, though the countryside can be unexciting. If Spain or Portugal is your target, the direct ferry (or even holding your nose and taking a plane) is the more practical option.

I haven't personally been to the **Balearics** (Majorca, Minorca and other islands), but I understand they're beautiful and have a lot of historic sites as well as the beaches. Ferry travel is a major attraction, and there are ferries to small islands not shown here.

The **Canary Islands**, off the southern tip of Morocco, are accessible by cruise-ferry from Cadiz. The journey takes two days and costs from £88, or £330 with a cabin. There are regular ferries between the islands, but nothing to the nearest land, Morocco.

The **Azores** are even further out, and there is no ferry service there.

Morocco is the safest destination in North Africa, but do your research if you plan to go there. The situation may change from year to year, and your personal situation might affect your choices. There are fascinating sights, and it has a great reputation for hospitality.

The Kasbah in Fez

Cheaper by coach

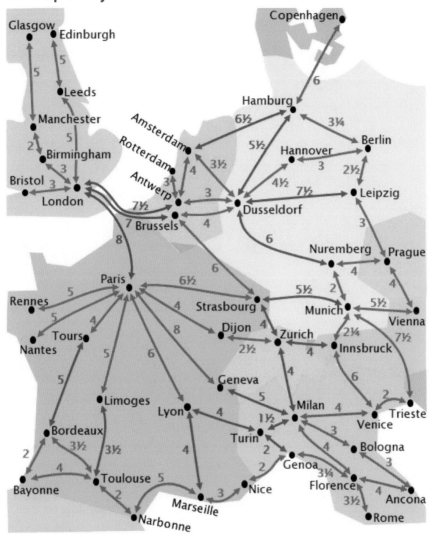

If you have more time (or less money) the long-distance coach network may work better than the train. Several coaches cross the channel, presumably by the Dover-Calais route, though the services don't commit to specific routes. They cut out a lot of the uncertainty of a normal foot-passenger crossing, as you simply board and debark on the car deck. No continental coaches run from anywhere else in England than London, but the Megabus and National Express networks connect at Victoria.

If you're heading for Spain or most of France, the Paris route makes the most sense, while either Brussels or Antwerp can be better for the Netherlands, Germany, or points east.

Image credit: Eddie on Flickr

Use the map as a guide to where you can travel in a day. In all cases, take the map only as a start. Because coaches are less frequent than trains, and often run at inconvenient times, it is best to put your whole route for the day into a website like Bus Radar and then compare times and prices. Shortest journey times aren't always the best fit. Because coaches take a long time to get into city centres, a direct one to your destination will generally be quicker than changing at an intermediate city. Notice that the Bus Radar search includes trains, which can be more expensive, and car-share schemes, which I've not tried. Watch out for coaches that terminate at airports, often a long way from the city and expensive to get out of.

Although the booking sites only show big-city bus stations, the coach may also stop in the suburbs. If you are staying overnight, those might be closer to cheap rooms, and you can take a tram or a local train into the city the following day. Go to the website of the coach operator, and click on the destination city for details.

Be prepared to show your passport if your bus crosses a national border. Even within the Schengen zone, bus companies are penalised if they carry illegal migrants, so they often check.

Most of the journeys on my map cost from €10 to €20, only a fraction of the cost of the train, but generally take at least twice as long. Unless you like overnight coaches, factor in the extra cost of overnight stays when calculating the overall cost.

Italy, Malta and Tunisia

Returning to trains now, this is the picture for Italy and
points south.

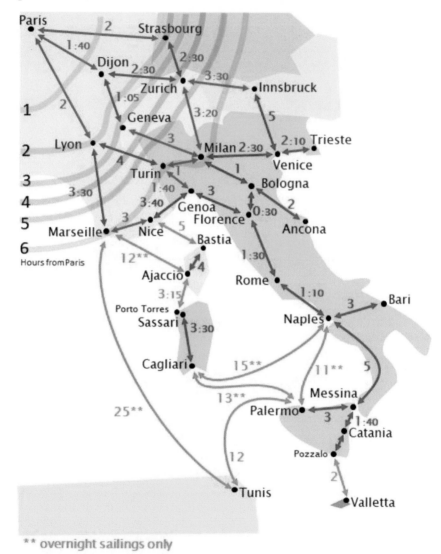

** overnight sailings only

Use this map for Italy, and also if you are heading for Malta,
Corsica, Sardinia and Tunisia. Adriatic destinations are
covered in *Central and Eastern Europe* on page 39.

Bastia, Corsica.

All roads may lead to Rome, but all railways to Italy seem to begin in Paris. So again, Dover-Calais is the fastest unless you live in the west of England. There is no advantage to taking any of the east-coast ferries, unless you live in the North and want to avoid London.

For any destination in Italy, neither the Strasbourg-Innsbruck nor the Marseille-Nice route have any time advantage, though they are both very beautiful. All the fastest routes pass through Milan. The Lyon-Turin route is about the same as the Dijon-Geneva one. Since all of these are too long to do in one day, you should choose a route based on where you want to stop along the way. Lyon and Dijon are worth a few days visit and there are many other stopping points to consider.

For me, the star attractions are the ancient ruins around Naples, at Pompeii and Herculaneum, but everywhere in Italy is steeped in history and much of it is very beautiful.

Herculaneum

The circumvesuviana railway, Naples

Mount Vesuvius

Volterra, near Perugia

Sicily, Corsica and
Sardinia all offer more
ferry opportunities, and
preserve a relaxed and
traditional lifestyle
much of the mainland
has forgotten.

Tunisia fell off the tourist map in 2015 when dozens of tourists were gunned down by a terrorist, but it is mostly safe these days. Outside the resort areas, much of the traditional lifestyle is preserved. There are also ruins from the time of ancient Rome, including the site where *The Life of Brian* was filmed. Check the FCO for the latest advice.

Monastir Ribat, near Sousse, by GIRAUD Patrick on Wikimedia

Equally fascinating, but unquestionably safe, is **Malta**, part of the British Empire for many years, and still very comfortable and welcoming for the English-speaking tourist.

Marsaxlokk, Malta

Valletta, Malta

Scandinavia and the Baltics

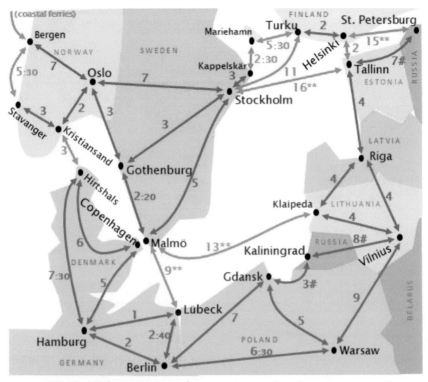

** overnight passages only
# Check visa requirements and safety issues for Russia

Hamburg is a gateway city for rail travel to anywhere on the Baltic. There used to be ferries to Esbjerg in Denmark and Stavanger in Norway, but these have gone. Hamburg and Kiel are within an easy day's journey of the East Coast ferries, and have a lot to see as well.

The Norwegian coast is a popular cruise-ship destination, starting in Stavanger or Bergen and going all the way to the Russian border outside Murmansk. See the operator Hurtigruten for details.

Image credit: <u>Richard Mortel</u> on Flickr

Their "Coastal" ships are also ferries for the locals up and down the fjords. Normally, they only call at an individual port for 15-30 minutes, but there are shore excursions that catch up with the ship at its next port. It looks as if it would also be possible to stay over in a port and join the next ship on the route. Check with the operator; you probably have to make detailed plans ahead of time. As well as the big ships, there are smaller ferries connecting to villages deeper into the fjords, so it sounds like a fascinating place to explore. Like all cruise-ships, they are not a cheap option.

The routes from Stockholm to Finland are a treat for ferry lovers, passing hundreds of rocky islands with antique cabins and boathouses, metres from the ship. Mariehamn, on Åland, provides opportunities for island-hopping on local buses and open car ferries, by stages to Turku.

All the Scandi countries are fascinating to visit, with a direct connection to our history. The murder rate is nowhere near what you might imagine from all the TV shows, the cities are full of museums, and everyone is friendly. Prices are relatively high, and the weather is challenging out of season.

King Gustav, Nordic Museum, Sotckholm

17th century ship Vasa, Stockholm

Each of the **Baltic** states is a different take on carving a unique identity out of a region that was for so long part of one empire or another. The Soviet past is remembered, as well as earlier domination by Poles, Teuton knights and whoever might be passing through with weapons.

Estonian Open Air Museum, Tallinn

Now they embrace membership in the EU and NATO, and are enthuiastic about democracy and freedom.

Trakai Castle, Lithuania

Maritime Museum, Riga

Central and Eastern Europe

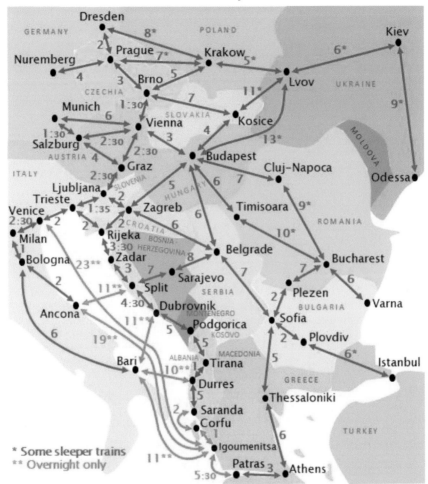

This region is vast and varied, from elegant historic cities like Vienna and Budapest, to the scenic beauty of the coast of Croatia. Travelling here is more of an adventure than in western Europe, and it's fascinating to see these places emerging from the gloomy Soviet era. Ljubljana, for example, is a pretty little city in a valley dominated by its old castle, with a youthful culture showing in street art and little cafes.

For lovers of ferries and history, it's hard to beat coastal Croatia. The sea is dotted with islands from 10km down to 1km, each with its own ferry from the mainland. All the ferries are run by one company, Jadrolinija. Their website will provide all the details you need, but they are frequent, and cost only a few Euros for a trip that would cost you €40 or more as a boat tour.

Split is the star attraction for me, with a historic centre weaving an ancient Roman palace with accretions and complications built on throughout the middle ages and up to the present day.

As a ferry-hopping hub, Šibenik is top. A lovely old city in itself, it looks much like Venice but on a hill.

Unije

Ferries from there run to the island of Unije, where cars are banned, and to the beautiful Stari Grad (old town) on Hvar.

Stari Grad, Hvar

All the cities on the coast are linked by frequent bus service, along coastal roads with spectacular views out to sea.

There used to be a coastal ferry all the way from Trieste to Corfu, but that has been cancelled. There are coastal cruises in small ships, if you can afford it.

If you are aiming for Greece, there is a lovely ferry from Venice direct to Igoumenitsa or Patra, taking 24 hours and passing beautiful islands. See page 57 for more on *Greece and the Aegean.*

Ireland

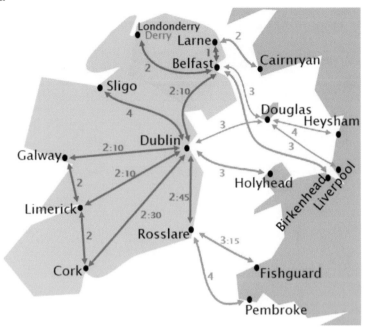

For timetables, see page 88. Routes shown here are the ones that take foot passengers. Additional routes may be possible by booking a through coach.

Ireland is a unique experience for the English traveller. The scenery is lovely, and the people are friendly. The whole Guinness-and-fiddle music thing is there, though perhaps not as prevalent as among Irish ex-pats around the world. Museums and attractions often mention the past sins of us Brits, but that's true in many places. The countryside is lovely and green, but there's a reason for that: it rains. A lot.

Northern Ireland is a zone of frozen conflict, of past wars suspended but not resolved. It seems very British, but in a rather retro fashion, with more small shops and less chain stores. Outside of central Belfast, the pace is slower and things seem a little run-down.

Image credit: Sitomon on Wikimedia

The unique aspect of the place, the scenes of sectarian violence and bigotry, seem too raw and disturbing to be treated as tourist attractions. Maybe in another few decades. The northern coast has spectacular scenery that may be a surprise.

Giant's Causeway, by Chmee2 on Wikimedia

Orkney and Shetland

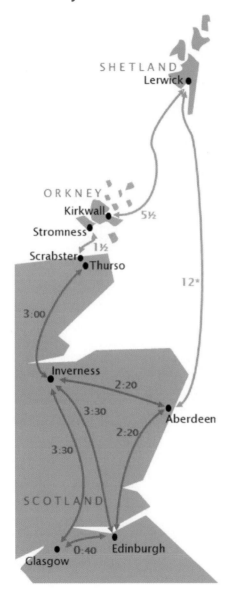

Not technically outside the UK, but definitely "overseas" are the remote Orkney and Shetland islands in the North Sea.

The ferry from Aberdeen is overnight, but quite economical, only £55 with a "sleep pod," which is an almost fully reclinable seat, with privacy wings. Cabins are available, but only for sharing.

Lerwick, Mike Pennington Geograph

Stromness, Guinog Wikimedia

Channel Isles

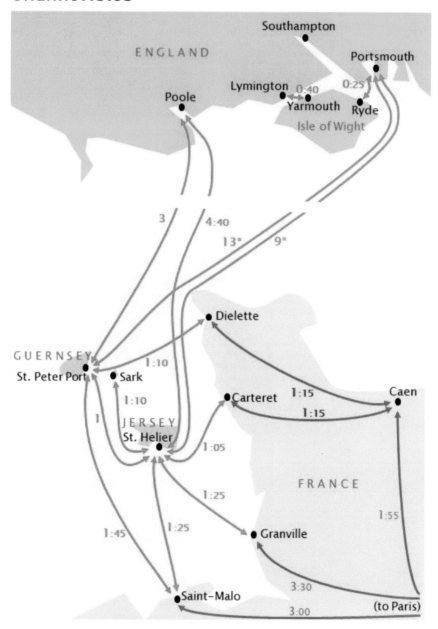

You may think of Jersey and Guernsey as places for rich
men to hide their money, so they won't have to pay taxes
like the rest of us. This is true, and it lends an air of luxury
and prosperity to the two main islands. But ordinary people

live there too, maintaining a mostly English lifestyle with a light dusting of French.

Castle Orgueil

St. Helier

Like Gibraltar, it's not quite foreign enough for me, but it's a place you can get to by ferry, and that has to be a good thing.

I've never been to the car-free island of Sark, but it seems like it would be worth a trip.

Sark Ferry at Guernsey

Cyprus

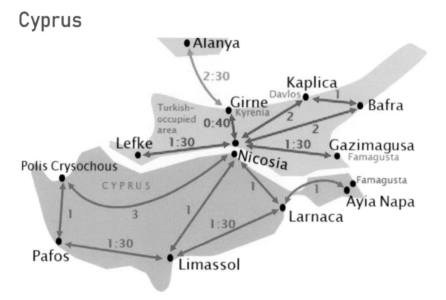

The island of Cyprus is divided by a hostile border. The internationally-recognised state of Cyprus, a member of the European Union, is open and safe. The northern part was invaded by Turkey in 1974, and they remain in occupation. A United Nations peacekeeping force maintains a border between them. Tourists on foot cross at a single crossing in the centre of Nicosia, a divided city.

Ottaman fort, Larnaca

The south is open and easy-going, with enormous resort hotels, huge swathes of villa and condo development, and thousands of ex-pats from the UK (and lately from Russia) loving the sun and watching their home football teams on screens at the pub. Buses there are easy to find, comfortable and cheap. Google Maps doesn't have data for these, but the official site at intercity-buses.com has all you need. They only run every few hours, so do plan ahead.

Signs suggest there may sometimes be trouble, even in the south, but I never saw any.

Limassol

Many Greek Cypriots were driven out of the north at the time of the invasion, now living as refugees in the south. This can lead to some confusion – buses headed for Famagusta don't go to the original city, which is now in the north, but to an area north of Ayia Napa where most of the refugees now live. You can take a boat tour from there to see the ghost city where many of those

people lived, though it only runs when it can find
passengers.

Promenade, Larnaca

The island is attractive enough for sun, sea and sand, but there
are spectacular cliffs and fascinating archaeological sites as well.

Cabo Greco

Tombs of the Kings, Pafos

Ayia Napia Monastery

There seems to be a ferry from Alanya in Turkey to the Turkish-occupied north at Kyrenia (Girne), but the normal ferry sites don't make bookings for this passage. Try a web search, and then e-mail or call the operator to confirm.

The northern part has a lawless feel, though I never felt unsafe there. Crossing on foot at the border post in Nicosia, you pass through the shopping district to a park, where buses tout for tourists for the two main destinations: Kyrenia (Girne in Turkish) and Famagusta (Gazimaguša). If you take one of these, they will sit you in a bus, but it may not be the one which is actually travelling, and it may be a while before the real one arrives.

Walk 500m to the north, to the bus station where the local people travel; you can see what's available there. Because of the confusion over Turkish, Greek and colonial British names, it's good to buy a map in the north, and check with the driver that he's heading where you want to go.

I really enjoyed visiting North Cyprus, but don't make plans on a tight schedule. Airbnb is available in the north, but read the descriptions carefully and don't take a dog or wear shoes in the house. The area is not part of the European Union, so make sure you have travel insurance and check with your insurer that it is valid there.

The most popular destination is Famagusta, a town where the ancient conflict between Christianity and Islam comes to the fore, most notably in the Norman churches, two in ruins and one long converted into a mosque.

The ferry from Turkey is not a mainstream tourist ship, so it's probably best to fly to the island. There are many cheap flights from the UK, or you can cut down air time by flying from Athens to Larnaca: £55, 1h40. There are also flights to the north, to Erkan near North Nicosia. These are cheaper, but only fly from Istanbul: £35, 1h30.

Israel

It is no longer possible to reach Israel by cruise-liner or ferry. See the discussion on the excellent rail travel website Seat 61. They mention a freight carrier that takes passengers there from Greece, but it is expensive and takes several days. Once upon a time you could take a train from Turkey to Israel, but the war has put a stop to that. There are direct flights from Luton (£160, 4h50) or from Athens (£60, 2h00).

The country has such a prominent place in religion, history and modern politics, many people are surprised how small it is. Practically, you could stay in Tel-Aviv or Jerusalem and visit most of the country on day trips. The exception is Eilat, in the south, but that is a seaside resort mostly visited by cheap flights from abroad. All the major religious and ancient sites are served by coach tours, but there are also local buses and trains.

To navigate safely and to understand what you are seeing, you need to know about the political divisions of the country. Israel proper is a modern democratic state with open institutions and a comfortable environment for foreigners. There are risks from terrorism, and there is a visible military presence in some areas, but it is generally safe and unrestricted. Take normal precautions such as staying with your luggage, but be extra vigilant. The one thing to watch out for is that there are holidays when all public transport shuts down, so check specific days in your itinerary when you plan your trip.

If you are a Jew or a Muslim, take particular care to research the rules before you travel. If you are travelling with local people, whether Arab or Jewish, be aware there are places where they are not allowed, even though you are. If you are neither of these, and you are asked your religion, say "Christian" regardless of how atheistic you may be. Don't assume that a western passport will exempt you from the rules; this is a place where religion and law are inextricably intertwined.

The West Bank, no matter how you feel about its politics, is a place where visitors need to be very careful. I personally advise against independent travel there, though people have tried it and had no problem. See TripAdvisor for more.

Jerusalem is divided, not just an Arabic east and a Jewish west, but into multiple areas, each with its own rules. Those rules apply differently depending on your nationality and religion, and they vary by month and day of the week.

Expect to see armed soldiers and police everywhere, and be prepared to stop if you walk down the wrong street. Remember that the eastern

part of the city, including the Anglican cathedral and the Mount of Olives area, are not in modern Israel, they are in East Jerusalem, with a similar status to the West Bank.

Bethlehem is the most popular tourist attraction in the West Bank itself. It is interesting from a religious/historical point of view, but it is also a good way to see an ordinary Arab village. Visits set out from Jerusalem, by organised coach tour or by a tourist taxi. Rather than taking an Israeli taxi in the Jewish quarter, you 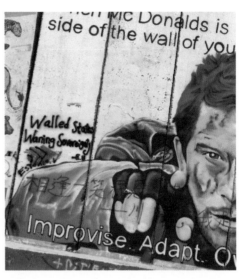 can walk across the old city to the Lion's gate and take an Arab taxi. The fare is agreed in advance: about £40 for a three-hour trip. The one I took came with a fair amount of political commentary, including a visit to the Arab side of the new concrete wall separating the West Bank, with graffiti rumoured to include a Banksy.

Masada

The ancient hill-fort of Masada and parts of the Dead Sea coast are in Israel proper, but most tours come from Jerusalem, passing through the West Bank on major roads. These tours come with more political commentary, this time from a Jewish perspective. Dedicated foot passengers can also visit independently from the southwest, via Be'er

Sheva. If you are not familiar with desert heat, take the cable car, carry litres of water, cover your head, and follow all the local advice. It is really, really hot.

Neighbouring countries are near-impossible to visit from Israel. The borders with Lebanon and Egypt are closed, and Syria and Gaza are war zones. The only notionally open border is the one with Jordan, where a few posts can be crossed, including this one near Eilat.

Photo Credit: NYC2TLV on Wikimedia

Israeli citizens are not allowed across, so there are no regular buses or trains. You do your research, take a taxi to the border, walk across and take another taxi to Amman or Petra. Opening times depend on both Jewish and Islamic holidays, and are different on the Sabbath. There are organised coach tours, to Petra in particular, but they are very expensive. Be aware that Jordanian border guards will stamp your passport with an entry from Israel, which may make it difficult for you to then enter any other Arab country. All in all, if you aim to visit Jordan, the easiest way is to fly in from Istanbul or Athens, not to combine it with a journey to Israel.

Greece and the Aegean

This looks like foot-passenger heaven, with all those connections to island harbours and historic towns. Unless you are flying in, the easiest way is one of the long voyages from Italy.

This can also be done by bus from Split, but some of the countries along the way are on my amber list, so check on safety and visa issues. I'm attempting this journey in May 2019, so check my website (or my obituary!).

The main tourist attractions on land are the ancient temples at Delphi and Olympia, and of course the Parthenon and the musuems of Athens. There are many more islands and many more ferries. The ones shown here give an overall impression: check Direct Ferries or the websites of the operators for more. Many ships only sail one or two days a week, so plan ahead or choose your destinations as you go.

Delphi

Every large island has a ferry direct from Piraeus; I've only shown a selection here. The timings are for fast ferries, usually catamarans. Slower ships are cheaper but may involve an overnight sailing, so check the trade-offs.

Land route timings are approximate: transport is by coach apart from the railway from Athens to Thessaloniki and across to Turkey. The coaches don't appear on Bus Radar and there's no central website for booking, so information is hard to get. The map shows car journey times in many cases, so allow more time for the actual trip. I'm pretty confident you can just turn up at a bus station and there will be a departure that day.

I'm unsure of the security and passport control situation between Greece and Turkey. They've never been the best of friends, and the situation is under more strain than usual with the regime in Turkey and the situation with migrants trying to cross into Europe. Plan ahead, allow a lot of time, and approach with care.

Image credit: <u>Reinhard Dietrich</u> on Wikimedia

Places without ferries

As we have shown, you can get anywhere in Europe by a combination of ferries, trains and coaches. There are one or two exceptions, though.

Iceland is on the itinerary of one or two cruise ships, notably the Princess Cruises tour that also includes the north coast of Norway. It's an expensive option though: at least £1900, more for single travellers. There is a short ferry across the bay near Reykjavik that also calls at a small flat island called Flatey. Which means 'Flat Island,' in Icelandic. Iceland is a treat for the geologically-inclined, as it's in the process of emerging out of a volcanic rift in the Atlantic. But it's a bit bleak, for me.

Sculptures near Keflavik

Greenland. See Iceland, only more so. Cruises there start at £2600, by Fred Olsen. The villages you visit often have less inhabitants than the ship itself, which must be an odd experience.

Switzerland and **Austria** are of course land-locked. The region is a paradise for train-lovers, with a different style of train, funicular or cable-car climbing every mountain in sight.

Brienz, Switzerland

Interlaken

If you're determined to arrive by water, though, it can be done, on a river cruise up the Rhine from Germany. The extremely well-advertised Viking Cruises are the most famous option, but there are others. River cruises are similar in cost to ocean ones, as the bulk of the cost is the hotel side. Plan on at least £1000 a week, if you're travelling alone, and expect industrial-strength guided tours ashore.

The Swiss lake steamers provide a more economical option, many of them historic, and reaching places inaccessible by road.

Iseltwald, near Interlaken

5 Accommodation

Choosing your Airbnb

On the surface, it's easy. Go to Airbnb.com, enter the name of the place you want to go, click on Homes, and you get a list. Bear in mind the list may include homes that are quite far from the centre, and the ones at the top of the list may be quite expensive. I go to 'filters' and choose a price limit (£30 in most of Europe, £20 in more obscure places) and then click on the map (a 📍 symbol in the phone app) to see how places are laid out. Look for the historic centre or the beach, wherever you expect to spend most time. If you are arriving late or leaving early, look for places near the station or ferry port, but those can be rough areas. You may have to zoom in a lot to concentrate on the area you want.

If you are unsure of an area, check it in street view in Google Maps, but be aware that run-down areas are not necessarily unsafe. I stayed in a lovely apartment in Sarajevo that looked like this from the street!

Suburbs or centre

The cheapest option is always to stay in the suburbs. It's quieter, you get more room for your money, and hosts usually have more time to help. On the other hand, it can be a struggle to get to the place, and you may have to navigate local transit after a long journey. You need to plan your travel to arrive early in the evening.

Many cities in Europe have towns within a 30-minute train ride that are lovely in themselves. If you stay there, you can commute to the big city any day, but have pleasant walks or tram rides in the surrounding area. I would always do this with cities like London, Paris or Milan, where city-centre accommodation is poor quality and expensive. Windsor, Potsdam and Versailles are all within 30 minutes of their cities, have their own attractions, and will save you 50% for your room.

Vaporetto leaving Punta Sabbioni, Lido di Jesolo

Better still, if you love boats, find a suburb reached by ferry from the city, like Punta Sabbioni for Venice or Sliema for Valletta.

Sliema Harbour Ferry, Malta

Private room or entire place

This is a very personal choice. If you feel uncomfortable walking around in pyjamas in a stranger's house, choose a self-contained flat or at least a room with an ensuite toilet. Always look carefully at the description to check the kitchen facilities. Not all "private room" setups allow kitchen privileges, and you can save a lot of money by eating in. I made this mistake on my present trip, and spent a week eating nothing but salad.

I can't emphasise enough, read the whole description and all of the reviews before you book. Some apartments listed as "entire place" clearly aren't so from the descriptions, and the reviews provide an insight into the professionalism of the host. Pay particular attention to reviews by women; I have seen places where the host has clearly hit on a woman travelling alone, and then tried to justify himself in his response to her review. "Run away, run away!"

At a more prosaic level, the description will tell you more about the accessibility of the place. I recently stayed in a flat in Genoa that was up the side of a cliff with 200 steps to get to it. OK for me, though tiring when carrying luggage, but it would be completely impossible for a person with motion difficulties.

If you have any concerns, message the host during the booking process. Ask if the place will work for you, and feel free to try somewhere else. Some places are marked for "instant booking," so the reservation will automatically be approved when you click on it. I prefer to avoid these, so there's some conversation with the host. However, be prepared to go through several tries. Hosts may be selecting guests on criteria they aren't talking about.

Short stays and late arrivals

If you're planning a short stay, check how easy it is to get to the apartment. Find one near the station or port, even if it costs a little more.

There are times when Airbnb may not be ideal. If you're arriving after 8pm, or staying only one night, a hotel may be a better choice. Expedia™ or any other travel agency site will provide a lot of options, even in out-of-the-way places. Outside of the big cities, even the cheapest hotels are usually fine.

Finding and arriving

Check any messages from the host before setting out for your room; don't rely on the information in the profile or that pin that gets dropped into Google Maps. Addresses are vague in places like Venice or Cyprus, but the host will be able to give exact directions.

If the host is not at home, you may need to find a key in a lockbox, or enter a code somewhere. I have found some places where the address is completely different from the one shown on the site – a student residence being rented out illegally, for example. For that one, the host met me in the Metro station, as if I were a spy.

If you find that the place is radically different from what you expected, don't hesitate to reject it. Airbnb will get a refund from the host, and there is always somewhere else you can stay. Don't pay the host extra cash – always pay through Airbnb, unless it's a very small amount. In Malta, for example, there's a €0.50/night tourist tax, which is not worth quibbling about.

In self-contained flats there is sometimes an electricity charge; you read the meter at the start and the end. Unlike the UK, there is no limit on the per-unit charge, and it may be up to €0.50 a unit. Pay that through Airbnb, but refuse it if it was not mentioned in the profile.

Think about your reviews

Airbnb is different from traditional consumer-oriented services. It is truly peer-to-peer: you evaluate your host, as on hotel booking sites, but they evaluate you right back. Get bad reviews, you may have trouble finding rooms. Get serious complaints and you may be kicked off the service altogether. That changes the relationship, in a good way.

So, be nice, clean up after yourself, and guys: don't hit on the hostess! They are operating a business, behave as you would (should!) in a workplace.

Homes hosted by women

Many homes on the Airbnb site appear to be hosted by women, but few turn out to be. This may be a marketing ploy. The owners may be a couple, or they may be lying. In some cases, it's a management company with hundreds of flats, and the named person is a manager. Some standalone apartments are hosted by people far away. I stayed in one in Cyprus where the host was in Russian-occupied Ukraine!

But... isn't Airbnb evil?

As the leading company in a market with a business model that cuts across existing cartels and conventions, Airbnb has attracted a lot of controversy. They've been accused of driving up rents for long-term residents, and "hollowing out" communities so everyone there is a transient. People say it encourages rowdy youth to treat their accommodation as "party flats." All I can say is that I've not experienced this personally, and most of the hosts I've stayed with have seemed genuine, ordinary people. In the same way that you can't blame an Uber passenger or their driver for the sins of that company, I think it's fair and reasonable for us and our hosts to use Airbnb.

In the articles I've seen on the social effects, Airbnb has been better than a lot of other room-finding services in cooperating with authorities and encouraging reasonable regulation of the sector. They point out that, unlike less formal ways of finding rooms, they have a traceable

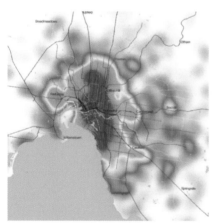

identification of both host and guest, and that they regularly cooperate with the authorities in cases where abuse is reported. They also encourage hosts to declare the income they receive, and collect local tourism taxes.

There's some interesting discussion on the Australian website City Metric, about this issue.

Airbnb room density for Wellington, Jacqui Alexander at City Metric

Disrupting established markets and creating more open ones will always harm some established players. Disintermediation means that people will lose their jobs if their only role is to mediate. Global, efficient markets increase the price of popular things. That's twenty-first century life. As consumers, all we can do is avoid things we consider unacceptable. I, personally, think Airbnb is an overall force for good. As citizens, we can encourage more regulation to control trends we find disturbing. Airbnb, on its record, is OK with that, as long as it's applied fairly.

As for those "party flats," I'm sure they're out there. I look for phrases like "great night life" and "in the centre of everything," and avoid them like the plague.

6 Travel

Eurail™ or Interrail™ passes

These are passes to provide "unlimited travel" on one or more days, on the entire European rail system. If you reside in the EU, they are called Interrail, from outside it's Eurail, but it is essentially the same deal. There are regular passes, which operate on consecutive days, or "Flex" passes, which allow non-consecutive days. For example, I bought a 3-day non-consecutive pass for £180, for my present trip. As you go through the booking process they pile on charges, and it ended up costing £205.

It's really nice having the freedom to get on a train at the drop of a hat, but it really is quite expensive. If I'd booked advance tickets for my Calais to Napoli trip, it would have cost about £180. But then I'd have been locked into a schedule. In the event, I decided to stay a different number of days, which wouldn't have been possible without a pass. However, pass holders pay for reservations on high-speed trains – up to €10 *per train* – and they are mandatory on the fastest ones.

Travelling out of season, you don't really need to book ahead. Unlike the UK system, where advance tickets are far cheaper, in most of Europe you get the same fare if you just turn up an hour or so before the trip. If it's not busy, you can just buy a ticket for each leg as you get to the station. The reservations are *mandatory*, but they aren't *necessary*, and you can buy minutes before the train leaves.

If you do have a pass, don't use a rail day for local travel. Trains and buses near cities are often very cheap. Rail passes are for long distances. Consider not using a rail day in countries where rail travel is very cheap, like Italy.

Coach

Coach travel is always the cheapest, though it may be slower. In most of Europe, Eurolines™ and Flixbus™ cover all major cities. They don't go every day, and the times may be inconvenient. Paris to Lyon is only €27, but the coach takes nearly seven hours and arrives very late in the evening. The train only takes two hours and offers several journeys a day, at prices from €40 to €80. Remember that late arrivals often mean spending more on accommodation. See my *Cheaper by coach* map on page 27 for more information, and use Bus Radar for planning.

Local travel

Don't rent a car for everyday touring, unless your destination is well outside a city. European cities are deliberately laid out to frustrate car users, to encourage commuters to leave the car at home. Use trams or metro[2] light rail for longer journeys, or walk where you can.

Groeningen, Netherlands

Don't assume you need to use public transport for everyday city touring. The metro is great for big cities, but in smaller ones you can walk anywhere you need to be.

I tend to be a bit wary of buses. Trams and light rail are easy; there's a map, and you can buy a ticket at a machine.

---

[2] I'm avoiding the American term "subway" to mean an underground railway. In European English, a subway is a pedestrian tunnel. It's "Underground" or "tube" in London, "metro" in most other places. In Germany or Scandinavia, it's "S-Bahn," for suburban railway.

Riga Market Halls

Bus routes are less obvious. In most places, you can't buy a ticket as you board. Don't rely too much on the numbers on buses and trams. Most routes go two ways through the city centre, and if you get on the wrong one you could be far away. If you can, get a day rover ticket that entitles you to free travel – usually, these cover all trams and buses. Then if you get on a bus going the wrong way, you get off and catch the one across the road.

If there's a central bus station, things are much clearer. There's a departure board with times, and usually a system map, too.

This is Valletta bus station, where a €1.60 ticket will get you anywhere in Malta.

In Italy, you buy a ticket at a *Tabacchi* kiosk, but remember to validate it when you board the bus. Insert the ticket into a machine near the door, usually yellow. You may have to tear a strip off the side of the ticket to make it fit. Most cities in France have a similar arrangement.

Local tours

Local tours are often overpriced. Use their itinerary to work out where to go, then use local buses and trains. It's far cheaper, and there's no annoying commentary. Example: Salerno to Sorrento, on the spectacular Amalfi coast in Italy, is £5 on local buses, £40 as a coach tour. And if you go it alone, you can make your own schedule.

Every city in Europe has an open-top bus tour. Ranging from €10 to €30, they give you a day ticket, and you can hop on and hop off at any of the sights.

Photo Credit: Dr. Avishai Teacher on Wikimedia.

In highly pedestrian cities, they miss out a lot of the sights because they simply aren't allowed down those streets. But they are usually a reasonable way to spend the day. Being a cheapskate, I generally take one of their brochures and use it to identify the best sights.

Palermo, Sicily

If the city has trams, a €5-day ticket will get you to all the places. If there are walking tours, take one of those, or likewise, glom off their itinerary. Don't follow them around listening in: that's rude.

If you are out of season in a city with few tourists, don't count on advertised tours actually being available. I was in Sarajevo in September 2016, and all the tours were €60, more than I am willing to pay. Talking to the young guys in the travel agency, it became clear they were simply going to hire me a cab for the day, to take me on whichever tour I picked.

7 Ferry timetables

Note: all these tables are gleaned from company websites on the day I was writing this section, and may contain errors. Please check with the company before making booking decisions. All schedules and costs for early May 2019. Winter choices may be more limited, summer costs higher.

Direct to Spain

	Plymouth	Portsmouth	
	Santander	Bilbao	Santander
Days of week	Su	We Su	Tu Fr Sa
Operator	Brittany	Brittany	Brittany
Edinburgh	-	12:30-1	08:30
Manchester	08:10	15:35-1	11:15
Birmingham	10:17	16:04-1	12:10
York	07:43	14:58-1	10:57
Cardiff	10:30	16:30-1	11:30
Bristol	11:44	17:23-1	12:22
London	10:03	05:30	14:00
UK station	14:10	07:25	15:55
Be at port	14:25	07:45	16:15
Depart	**15:25**	**08:45 D**	**17:15**
Arrive	12:15+1	14:15+1	18:15+1 **E**
Main station	12:25+1	16:00+1 **Q**	18:25+1
Cost*	£184	A	£150
Cost F	**£184**	**A**	**£180**
Pamplona	17:39+1	20:30+1 **N**	-
Madrid	18:38+1	21:12+1 **N**	-
Barcelona	20:40+1 **N**	23:40+1 **N**	-

* Single foot passenger, including cabin.
A No price quoted on website.
D Early start. Consider staying overnight near Portsmouth.
E Late arrival. Consider staying overnight near Santander.
F Including cost of overnight stay where indicated.

N Late night arrival. Consider hotel rather than Airbnb.

Q No public transport, the metro is 3km away. Consider a
      taxi.

For most of England the Portsmouth-Santander route saves
a lot of travel in the UK, but note that the late arrival means
staying over in or near Santander. These ferries are not
cheap, but they cut out travel through France, and the cost
of this needs to be factored into your decision.

Unless you are aiming to see Bilbao itself, there is no
advantage to the Portsmouth-Bilbao route. Even for
Pamplona, the earlier arrival of the Santander ferries means
you can get there on the same day, while the Bilbao arrival
is in the evening.

Santander

The Bay of Biscay can be rough if there's a storm in the area.

Plymouth to Roscoff

Days of week	Plymouth	Roscoff	
	Tu Fr Su	Tu Fr Su	Mo We Sa
Operator		Brittany	
Edinburgh	12:50-1	12:50	-
Manchester	15:10-1	15:10	07:10
Birmingham	17:12-1	17:12	09:17
York	14:44-1	14:44	06:45
Cardiff	17:30-1	17:30	10:30
Bristol	18:45-1	18:45	11:44
London	18:03-1	18:03	10:03
UK station	06:45	21:45	13:45
Be at port	07:00	22:00	14:00
Depart*	**08:00 D**	**23:00**	**15:00**
Arrive	15:00	07:30+1	21:30 **EN**
Main station	15:10	07:40+1	21:40
Cost*	£39	£90 B	£39
Cost F	**£69**	**£90**	**£69**
Paris	20:04	13:04+1	13:04+1
Bordeaux	23:59 **N**	19:52+1	19:52+1
Strasbourg	22:13 **N**	15:41+1	15:41+1
Milan	-	21:50+1**N**	21:50+1**N**

*	Single foot passenger, including cabin if overnight.
B	Includes cabin for single traveller. Cheaper for couples or groups.
D	Early start. Consider staying overnight near UK port.
E	Late arrival. Consider staying overnight near overseas port.
F	Includes £30 at either end for B&B stay.
N	Arriving very late. Consider using a hotel, rather than an Airbnb or guest house.

Plymouth departures make sense if you live in the west country or you aim to visit Brittany. Otherwise, you can save time and money by sailing from Portsmouth or other ports.

Cabins are expensive on this route; you can certainly save money by taking a daytime sailing and staying overnight at either end.

Brunel's Tamar bridge, by <u>Graham Richardson</u> on Flickr

Roscoff Harbour, by <u>Giorgio Galeotti</u> on Wikimedia

Poole to Cherbourg

	Poole		
		Cherbourg	
Days of week	Tu Th Su	Mo We Fr Sa	Mo We Fr
Operator		Brittany	
Edinburgh	-	11:30	11:30-1
Manchester	06:58	14:15	14:15-1
Birmingham	08:04	15:04	15:04-1
York	06:31	14:06	14:06-1
Cardiff	07:56	15:56	15:56-1
Bristol	08:41	15:30	16:48-1
London	09:35	17:05	19:05-1
UK station	12:10	19:40	07:05
Be at port	12:35	20:05	07:30
Depart*	**13:45**	**21:15**	**08:30 D**
Arrive	19:15 **E**	07:00+1	13:45
Main station	19:55	07:40+1	14:25
Cost**	£30	£105 **B**	£30
Cost F	**£60**	**£105**	**£60**
Paris	10:49+1	10:49+1 **J**	19:18
Bordeaux	13:56+1	13:56+1 **J**	21:48 **N**
Strasbourg	14:41+1	17:09+1	22:13 **N**
Milan	20:32+1**N**	21:50+1**N**	-

* Single foot passenger, including cabin if overnight

B Includes single cabin. Cheaper for couples or groups.

D Early start. Consider staying overnight near Poole.

E Late arrival. Consider overnight stay near Cherbourg.

F Includes £30 at either end for B&B stay

J Requires a tight connection at Cherbourg. Consider taking a taxi, or a later train.

N Arriving very late. Consider using a hotel, rather than an airBnb or guest house.

This is a reasonable route, but it costs a little more than Portsmouth for little advantage in time, and cabins are expensive.

Portsmouth routes (daytime)

For overnight sailings, see page 80.

	Portsmouth				
	Cherbourg	Caen		Le Havre	
Days of week	(daily)	(daily)	(daily)	Tu Fr Su	Mo Th Sa
Operator	Brittany				
Edinburgh	12:30-1	12:30-1	05:40	12:30-1	06:56
Manchester	15:35-1	15:35-1	08:15	15:35-1	09:15
Birmingham	16:04-1	16:04-1	09:30	16:04-1	09:30
York	14:58-1	14:58-1	08:57	14:58-1	09:30
Cardiff	16:30-1	16:30-1	09:30	16:30-1	10:30
Bristol	17:23-1	17:23-1	10:22	17:23-1	11:22
London	05:30 **S**	18:09-1	12:00	18:09-1	12:09
Portsmouth	07:35	06:50	13:25	06:35	14:05
Be at port	08:00	07:15	13:45	07:00	14:30
Depart	**09:00 D**	**08:15 D**	**14:45**	**08:00 D**	**15:30**
Arrive	13:00	15:00	21:30 **N**	14:30	22:00 **N**
Main station	13:20	15:45	22:15 **G**	14:40	22:10 **G**
Cost*	£35	£35	£35	£30	£30
Cost F	**£65**	**£65**	**£65**	**£60**	**£60**
Paris	16:49	19:14	10:00+1	18:14	09:17+1
Bordeaux	19:56	-	-	21:48 **N**	12:56+1
Madrid	-	-	-	-	22:06+1**N**
Strasbourg	22:13 **N**	22:13 **N**	12:41+1	22:13 **N**	12:41+1
Milan	-	-	18:35+1	-	18:35+1
Cologne	-	-	-	-	14:15+1
Hannover	-	-	-	-	19:18+1
Hamburg	-	-	-	-	21:02+1**N**

*   Single foot passenger, no cabin.

D   Early start. Consider staying overnight near Portsmouth.

F   Includes £30 for B&B stay

G   Public transport may not run this late. Consider a taxi.

N   Arriving very late. Consider using a hotel, rather than an airBnb or guest house.

S   Early start. Overnight stay may not be needed.

Portsmouth offers a wider variety of destinations than any other port, and is easier to get to than Plymouth for sailings to Normandy or Brittany. It's quicker to reach by rail than Dover, unless you are starting in London.

Portsmouth Naval Dockyard

Image credit: <u>Cherbourg Tourist Office</u> on Wikimedia

Portsmouth routes (overnight)

For daytime sailings, see page 78.

	Portsmouth		
	St. Malo	Caen	Le Havre
Days of week	**not** Tu Th	(daily)	**not** Sa
Operator	Brittany		
Edinburgh	11:30	12:30	12:30
Manchester	13:55	15:35	15:35
Birmingham	15:04	16:04	16:04
York	14:06	14:58	14:58
Cardiff	14:30	16:30	16:30
Bristol	15:22	17:23	17:23
London	16:36	18:09	18:09
UK station	18:50	20:20	21:35
Be at port	19:15	21:45	22:00
Depart	**20:15**	**22:45**	**23:00**
Arrive	08:15+1	06:45+1	06:45+1
Main station	08:45+1	07:30+1	06:55+1
Cost*	**£94**	**£90**	**£105**
Paris	11:23+1	10:47+1	10:15+1
Bordeaux	13:56+1	14:52+1	12:56+1
Strasbourg	14:11+1	14:21+1	13:22+1
Milan	20:10+1**N**	20:10+1**N**	17:15+1
Cologne	-	15:15+1	15:15+1
Hannover	-	19:01+1	18:17+1
Hamburg	-	19:46+1	19:35+1

* Single foot passenger, including cabin. Cheaper for couples or groups.

N Arriving very late. Consider using a hotel, rather than an Airbnb or guest house.

Not the cheapest route by any means, but trains connect Portsmouth to most of England without passing through

London, and the early start on the French side means you can get to all of France, much of Germany and Switzerland on the day you arrive. Even Milan is possible from Le Havre, though that's a very long day to be sitting in trains.

Photo credit: <u>Matt Hance</u> on Flickr

Newhaven to Dieppe

	Newhaven		
	Dieppe		
Days of week	(daily)	(daily)	(daily)
Operator	DFDS	DFDS	DFDS
Edinburgh	13:30-1	09:30	13:30
Manchester	15:35-1	11:35	15:35
Birmingham	16:10-1	12:10	16:10
York	16:03-1	11:58	16:03
Cardiff	15:56-1	11:56	15:56
Bristol	17:31-1	14:00	17:31
London	05:44 **S**	14:46	19:46
Gatwick ✈	06:42 **S**	15:20	20:20
Newhaven	07:55	16:25	21:55
Be at port	08:00	16:30	22:00
Depart*	**09:00 DK**	**17:30 K**	**23:00**
Arrive	14:00	23:00 **EN**	05:00 +1
Dieppe	14:30	23:30	05:30 +1
Cost	£23	£23	£63 **B**
Cost F	**£53**	**£53**	**£63**
Paris	18:14	08:41+1	08:41+1
Bordeaux	21:48	12:56+1	12:56+1
Madrid	-	22:06+1 **N**	22:06+1 **N**
Strasbourg	22:13 **N**	11:13+1	11:13+1
Milan	-	21:50+1 **N**	18:35+1
Cologne	-	15:15+1	15:15+1
Hannover	-	18:17+1	18:17+1
Hamburg	-	19:35+1	19:35+1

   * All schedules and costs for early May 2019. Winter choices may be more limited, summer costs higher.

   B Includes cabin for single traveller. Cheaper for couples or groups.

   D Early start. Consider staying overnight near UK port.

   E Late arrival. Consider staying overnight near overseas port

   F Includes £30 at either end for B&B stay where shown.

K Departures and prices vary from day to day, table shows best prices and typical times.

N Arriving very late. Consider using a hotel, rather than an airBnb or guest house.

S Same-day early start. Ignore the overnight stay at the ferry port.

This is the least expensive ferry across the channel, and cabins on the overnight sailing are also very reasonable.

Translink ferry at Newhaven: <u>*grassroots groundswell*</u> *Wikimedia*

Both ports are much closer to their main stations, and more foot-passenger friendly. They are also nice places to stay, if you decide on an overnight stop at either end. Highly recommended.

This book is mostly aimed at people living in the Britain, but it's worth noting that Newhaven is very close to Gatwick, if you're flying in from somewhere else.

Cliffs near Newhaven: <u>*Oast House Archive*</u> *on Geograph*

Dover routes

	Dover				
	Calais				Dunkirk
Days of week	(daily)	(daily)	(daily)	(daily)	(none)
Operator ፕ	P & O	P & O	P & O	P & O	DFDS
Edinburgh	13:30-1	-	05:40	09:30	-
Manchester	15:55-1	05:55	07:55	11:55	-
Birmingham	16:50-1	06:50	08:50	12:50	-
York	16:03-1	05:59	08:21	12:02	-
Cardiff	15:26-1	05:55	07:56	11:26	-
Bristol	16:00-1	06:00	08:10	12:00	-
London	04:37 **S**	08:37	10:37	14:37	-
Dover Priory	06:25	10:05	12:35	16:45	-
Be at port	07:25	11:05	13:35	17:45	-
Depart*	**08:25 D**	**12:05 LR**	**14:05 L**	**18:45 L**	**M**
Arrive	10:10	14:35	16:35	21:15 **EN**	-
Calais-Fréthun	12:10	16:35	18:35	22:15 **EN**	-
Cost	£30	£30	£30	£30	-
Cost F	**£60**	**£30**	**£30**	**£60**	**-**
Paris	14:14	18:14	20:14 **N**	09:14+1	-
Bordeaux	16:56	21:48 **N**	-	12:56+1	-
Madrid	-	-	-	22:06+1**N**	-
Strasbourg	17:15	20:41 **N**	-	12:41+1	-
Milan	22:05 **N**	-	-	18:35+1	-
Cologne	18:15	20:15 **N**	-	10:15+1	-
Hannover	17:28	22:28 **N**	-	17:28+1	-
Hamburg	-	-	-	19:35+1	-

* All schedules and costs for early May 2019. Winter choices may be more limited, summer costs higher.
ፕ Several companies operate from Dover, and more choices are available.
D Early start. Consider staying overnight near Dover.

E Late arrival. Consider staying overnight near Calais.

F Includes £30 at ferry ports for B&B stay.

L There are several departures throughout the day. Only examples are shown. Dover ferries are not suitable for overnight travel.

M Foot passengers are not allowed on this route, due to security issues caused by migrants.

N Arriving very late. Consider using a hotel, rather than an Airbnb or guest house.

R A Flixbus coach offers a similar schedule for less. £18 from London (0800) to Paris (1730). See Cheaper by Coach.

S Same-day early start. Ignore the overnight stay at the ferry port.

Dover-Calais offers a large variety of sailings and has a huge capacity, but it is not very friendly to foot passengers. The port of Calais is surrounded by high razor-wire fences designed to keep out migrants, and the high-speed station of Calais-Fréthun is a two-mile walk and a 20-minute train ride from where the bus drops you off.

There are trains from Calais-Ville, but they are not efficient, and definitely not very pretty.

East coast routes

	Harwich		Hull		Newcastle
	Rotterdam		Zeebrugge	Rotterdam	Amsterdam
Days of week	(daily)	(daily)	(daily)	(daily)	(daily)
Operator	Stena	Stena	P & O	P & O	DFDS
Edinburgh	14:30-1	14:30	13:30	13:30	13:30
Manchester	16:35-1	16:35	15:47	15:47	12:32
Birmingham	17:30-1	17:30	15:03	15:03	-
York	17:06-1	17:06	16:25	16:25	13:54
Cardiff	16:26-1	16:26	-	-	-
Bristol	17:00-1	17:00	-	-	-
London	19:32-1	19:32	-	-	-
UK station	07:55	21:55	18:20 **E**	18:20 **E**	14:45 **G**
Be at port	08:00	22:00	19:00	19:00	16:00
Depart*	**09:00 D**	**23:00**	**20:30 K**	**20:30 K**	**17:00**
Arrive	17:15	08:00+1	08:30+1	08:30+1	09:45+1
Main station	18:00	08:45+1	09:10+1	09:15+1	10:15+1 **P**
Cost**	£40	£75 **C**	£124 **C**	£124 **C**	£111 **C**
Cost F	**£70**	**£75**	**£124**	**£124**	**£111**
Paris	21:38 **N**	11:38+1	14:35+1	11:38+1	14:35+1
Bordeaux	-	14:56+1	17:56+1	14:56+1	17:56+1
Madrid	-	-	-	-	-
Strasbourg	-	14:41+1	14:41+1**J**	15:41+1	17:09+1
Milan	-	20:32+1**N**	21:37+1**JN**	21:37+1**N**	22:37+1**N**
Cologne	21:12 **N**	12:15+1	14:15+1	12:15+1	13:15+1
Hannover	-	15:18+1	17:28+1	15:18+1	15:18+1
Hamburg	-	18:35+1	18:53+1	18:35+1	16:14+1

   * All schedules and costs for early May 2019. Winter choices may be more limited, summer costs higher.

  ** Single foot passenger, including cabin if overnight.

   B Includes cabin for single traveller. Cheaper for couples or groups.

   C Price varies by sailing day. Check operator website.

D Early start. Consider staying overnight near UK port.

E The bus from Hull Paragon Interchange leaves at 17:00. After this time, take a taxi as local buses don't serve the terminal.

F Includes £30 for B&B stay at Harwich.

G The DFDS bus from Newcastle station leaves at 14:45 or 15:45. After this time, take a taxi as local buses don't serve the terminal.

J Requires a tight connection at the port. Consider taking a taxi

K Departures and prices vary from day to day, table shows best prices and typical times.

N Arriving very late. Consider using a hotel, rather than an Airbnb or guest house.

P The ferry company operates dedicated city centre buses at both ends (extra cost)

Felixtowe harbour and a cargo ferry, at Harwich

Not the cheapest options by any means, but if you are starting in the north or east it can save a lot of travel in the UK. If you are heading for the Netherlands, Germany or points east, again these routes cut out a lot of travel.

The Harwich day sailing is long, with an early start and a late arrival, good only for destinations in the Netherlands. These operators ask you to turn up very early, and the ports are in industrial cargo zones. Use the dedicated bus, and check the operator for times.

Eurpoort Rotterdam, by Quistnix on Wikimedia

Ireland from Wales

For other routes to Ireland, see page 90.

Days of week	Pembroke		Fishguard		Holyhead	
	Rosslare				Dublin	
	(daily)				(daily) J	
Operator T	Irish Ferries		Stena		Stena/Irish	
Edinburgh	13:55-1	-	-	12:00	17:31-1	12:13-1
Manchester	17:30-1	06:29	-	15:31	21:50-1	14:52-1
Birmingham	18:30-1	07:42	-	16:42	21:15-1	14:36-1
Newcastle	15:24-1	-	-	13:35	19:05-1	12:18-1
York	16:25-1	04:40 E	-	14:35	20:09-1	13:21-1
Cardiff	21:10-1	10:04	06:39	19:04	19:34-1	13:21-1
Bristol	19:54-1	08:45	-	17:54	19:30-1	12:54-1
London	18:33-1	07:45	-	16:46	19:01-1	14:10-1
UK station	01:25 C	13:25 C	11:35 H	22:10 H	01:20 L	07:15 L
Be at port	01:45	13:45	11:40	22:15	01:30	07:25
Depart	02:45	14:45	13:10	23:45	02:30 K	08:55
Arrive	06:46	18:46	16:25	04:00+1	05:55	12:10
Main station	06:55 D	18:55 D	16:35 D	04:20+1 D	06:00 N	12:15 P
Cost	£87 A	£33	£33	£33 G	£69 A	£33
Cost	£87	£33	£33	£33	£69	£63 M
Dublin	10:00	21:30 F	19:14	08:20+1	06:33 N	12:42
Cork	11:15	23:15 F	21:45 F	10:15+1	09:30 N	16:35
Limerick	11:05	23:15 F	21:10 F	11:05+1	09:04 N	16:08
Galway	13:15	-	22:15 F	11:45+1	10:08 N	17:58
Sligo	14:15	-	23:40 F	12:15+1	10:15 N	18:06
Belfast	12:35	-	22:50 F	11:50+1	09:45 N	15:35

A Including cabin for single passenger. Cheaper for couples or groups.

B Including B&B cost near ferry port, where required.

C Times are for Pembroke Dock station, but there are few trains. Take Megabus from Newport or Cardiff, or a local bus from Milford Haven.

D Times for Rosslare Europort station, but there is no evening or night train from there. Take the local bus to Wexford.

E Very early start. Consider staying overnight nearer the port.

F Very late arrival. Use a hotel rather an Airbnb or a guest house.

G No cabins are offered on this overnight ferry.

H Times shown are for *Fishguard and Goodwick* station. Don't use *Fishguard Harbour*.

J Additional sailings on some days.

K Stena sails at 02:30, Irish Ferries at 02:40.

L Times for Holyhead Port station.

M Cost including £30 for overnight stay in Holyhead.

N Times are for Dun Laoghoire station, which has no night trains. Consider a taxi or a local bus.

P Times are for Dun Laoghoire station.

All the ferries on these routes seem to run at inconvenient times, sailing in the small hours of the morning or arriving too late for onward trains. Consider the Liverpool or Scottish routes before deciding on a ferry.

Fishguard Harbour, by Paul Larkin on Wikimedia

Ireland from the north

	Liverpool	Birkenhead			Cairnryan	
	Dublin	Belfast			Larne	Belfast
Days of week	**A**	- - - - (daily) - - - - -				**A**
Operator T	P & O	Stena			P & O	
Edinburgh	-	15:30	-	16:00	15:12-1	-
Glasgow	-	15:40	-	17:30	16:28-1**K**	-
Manchester	-	18:55	06:57	19:55	14:26-1	-
Birmingham	-	18:01	06:01	19:36	13:15-1	-
Newcastle	-	17:03	-	17:26	14:15-1	-
York	-	17:38	05:38	18:41	13:02-1	-
Cardiff	-	16:21	-	18:21	10:50-1	-
Bristol	-	16:30	-	18:00	11:30-1	-
London	-	16:02	-	18:02	11:00-1	-
UK station	-	20:45 **F**	08:45 **F**	22:15 **F**	06:25 **G**	-
Be at port	-	21:00	09:00	22:30	07:00	-
Depart	**-**	**22:30**	**10:30**	**23:59**	**07:30**	**-**
Arrive	-	06:30+1	18:30	01:59+1	09:30 **H**	-
Belfast	-	07:39	19:05	2:30+1**J**	12:00	-
Cost	-	£95 **B**	£30	£27 **C**	£27	-
Cost	**-**	**£95**	**£30**	**£67 E**	**£57 D**	**-**
Dublin	-	10:00	21:40 **K**	10:00+1	13:38	-
Cork	-	12:30	-	12:30+1	16:35	-
Limerick	-	12:42	-	12:42+1	16:08	-
Galway	-	13:15	-	13:15+1	16:45	-
Sligo	-	13:32	-	13:32+1	17:32	-

A No foot passengers allowed. May be used by booking a through coach. See operator websites.

B Including cabin cost. Cheaper for couples or groups.

C No cabins are provided on this sailing.

D Cost includes B & B stay in Stranraer.

E Cost including hotel stay in Belfast. Too late for B & B.

F Birkenhead Hamilton Square station.

G Stranraer Station. Use bus 350 for the ferry port on weekdays, taxi on Sunday.

H Larne Harbour Station.

J No night buses. Use a taxi.

K There is a bus from Glasgow direct to the Cairnryan ferry terminal, but it must be booked two days ahead. See Scottish Citylink for details.

8 Foreign parts

Speaking the language

We tend to think of English as a universal second language, and it's true at a certain level of society. If you're having a meeting with business people, you can generally count on fluency. But we're travelling in poorer places, and meeting people who are not part of the corporate tourist industry, so we meet more non-English speakers.

In the Netherlands and Scandinavia, you can count on people speaking English as a matter of course.

In France outside Paris and in Spain, English is not widespread at all. They may have learned it in school, but like an English person's French, it can be rather useless. The same applies in Germany: outside the big cities, you are on your own.

In Italy, English is quite rare. They learn French in school, so you may have better luck with that.

Queen Vic pub, Pafos

Special cases are Malta and Cyprus, which had varying degrees of British government in the past, and are still part of the commonwealth. English is widespread, and very good. Maltese people are often educated in English, which is highly accented but completely fluent.

In all of Eastern Europe, young people speak English. Older people may speak Russian, which is unlikely to help you.

You'll always have better luck with younger people, and the staff in tourist offices and souvenir shops always speak English.

I have a standard phrase "I'm sorry, I don't speak (language)" which I use if someone speaks to me. Even if they don't understand what I say, it gets the idea across. I had a funny conversation in Copenhagen, where a lady said

something to me, and (lacking subtitles) I said "I'm sorry I don't speak Danish."

She said, "nor do I, I was speaking Swedish." In perfect English, of course. She wanted to know the way to the station, but I was lost, too. This was before Google Maps.

Wherever you are, you need to keep things simple. If you want tickets to somewhere by rail, simply say the name of the place. If you're not confident of the pronunciation, write it down or point to it on a map. Don't try to make a sentence out of it. The same with food: don't say "What ho, good man, do you have any ripe bananas?" Just say "banana."

Wherever you go, learn the words for good-day, goodbye, please and thankyou. In places where little English is spoken, learn yes/no, open/closed, today/tomorrow, and some numbers.

It's worth noting that the word "Euro" won't be recognised if you pronounce it "you row," as Brits tend to do. It's closer to "aero" in most languages, and even fluent English-speakers say it that way.

You may need to recognise signs for push/pull, exit/entrance, town centre, old town, ticket, office, train, bus and station.

Failing that, Google Translate does a great job. Get the app on your phone, download the dictionary for the language you need, and type in what you want to say.

One more language-like issue: smiling and nodding gets you a long way in most countries, but beware of it in Turkey or Arab countries. Nodding the head there means "no."

©™ Google

Ferry life

Naples-Palermo Ferry

Always bring packed meals and bottled water. Prices for meals and snacks on ferries are at least twice what you would pay ashore. If you need milk for cereal, buy a small pack of UHT – it doesn't need to be cooled as long as it is unopened. An extreme example of this is P&O Ferries between Dover and Calais. Fish and chips is £5.99 in the lorry drivers' café, £11.99 in the place where other victims have to eat. Take a sandwich, it's not a long sailing.

This is a high-end outside cabin, on MV Highlander. You will more commonly get four bunks in a cabin this size, and no window unless you pay extra.

Image credit: Loozrboy on Flickr

Food shopping

If you shop in UK supermarkets, you're used to fresh produce being weighed at the till when you check out. This can cause trouble in some parts, especially south of the Alps.

In those places, there is a weighing machine near the produce, and each type of fruit or veg has a code. Pick what you want, bag it and put it on the weighing machine. Enter the code, and the machine prints a label, which you stick on the bag.

Photo Credit: Santeri Viinamäki on Wikimedia

Another peculiarity of UK supermarkets is the effort they take to have the same produce on the shelf any time of the year. Brits like green beans, which have a growing season of about three weeks, but they are on our shelves all year, flown in from Kenya or Thailand. Italians are much more accepting of the idea that every food has a season, so you may have to expand your horizons a little. I'm in Sicily in February at present, and in the habit of buying grapes whenever I can. No grapes. But all kinds of oranges are abundant and extremely cheap, so I'm getting those.

Supermarket stuff isn't the best quality, especially in poorer countries, but the advantage is that you don't have to talk.

Šibenik, Croatia

Street markets and bakeries are easy, just point at what you want. But I tend to avoid butcher shops and the like. In former communist countries there are huge produce markets that have excellent stuff and are an entertainment in themselves. But they are often for local farmers. If you want bananas you may be out of luck, though they sometimes have them hidden under the stall.

Communist service

Many countries in Eastern Europe have customer service habits they learned under the Russians. They seldom smile or say please and thank you. Don't take it personally, it's just their way. England was the same, in the seventies.

Zinnowitz, near Peenemünde, Germany

You are also more likely to come across ticket-based queueing, in post offices, bus stations, and even some railway stations. If people are standing around in a crowd instead of queuing, look for a ticket machine. Take a numbered ticket, and watch for displays over the counter. If they are just shouting out the numbers (and you don't understand), try showing your ticket to someone else, they can probably let you know when it's your turn.

Places to avoid?

Is it OK to go to Venice or Florence? This may seem like a silly question, as millions of people visit there every year. But that's the problem, for me.

Florence

These places have lost nearly all of their original residents, and those that remain curse us tourists for clogging up their streets with our ugly clothes and overweight bodies. I love Venice, and can't resist going there often, but I go far out of season when the weather is bad, and steer clear of St. Mark's square and the Rialto, where you can't move without being hit with a selfie-stick. On the other hand, do **not** go to Venice during Acqua Alta, their annual flood season.

St. Mark's Square, Venice, by Giovanni Mello.

It is a disaster for them, and dealing with gawking tourists just adds to the stress. Check the forecasts at the <u>City of Venice site</u> and change your plans if the graph is over 100cm.

In Florence, the main hazard is large groups of American high-school students, accompanied by loud guides. Choose a time when these won't be around – they don't finish their pancakes until 10:00.

The fine-art galleries are the main attraction there, operating on a timed ticket system. A few days before you expect to arrive, go to the city website and book your time. Then you can bypass the long queues. In peak season, you should book museum tickets several days ahead.

The queue to climb the tower of the Duomo is not bookable, you'll just have to wait.

See visitflorence.com for more.

Learn local names

Learn the local names of cities, as the English term may not
be well understood and will cause confusion.

Venice	Venezia	Venet-see-uh
Florence	Firenze	Fear-ent-she
Naples	Napoli	Nah-pole-ee
Cologne	Köln	Kerln
Munich	München	Moon-shun
Vienna	Wien	Veen

Limit what you pack

Travelling this way, access may be more difficult. A flat may
be on the sixth floor with no lift, trains have steep steps and
low platforms. So, limit bags to one day-pack you can easily
keep on your lap and a wheelie carry-on bag. Mine has an
expansion zip for times when I have too much stuff, but
opening that may make it too big for the stingier airlines. If
you're buying a bag, look for one with large, soft wheels, as
you'll be wheeling along cobbled streets. Don't use a large
backpack; people on trams hate having them in their faces,
and it marks you out as a different kind of traveller.

Take e-books, not
paper ones. You will
probably read more, as
TV is all in other
languages and most
streaming sites don't
work. This is sensible
advice I generally
ignore, because I like
to read books that
predate the internet. I
trade off by taking
fewer clothes, but still
my bags are heavy. By
the way, Netflix does work in any country, but you'll see a
different selection of programmes.

If you're self catering, take plastic self-seal containers
(Tupperware). It's not possible to use up everything each
time you move, so you'll be wasting food otherwise. Of

course, your main bag will need room for these, as you don't want to be carrying a shopping bag along with your travel bags.

Make sure you have chargers for any electronics you take, and adapters for the round Euro socket at least. Older apartments may have pre-Euro sockets, but the host or a nearby shop will have an adapter. There's no issue with voltage; it's 220 volts everywhere. See worldstandards.EU for exhaustive detail.

Keep an ongoing list of things to pack – I tend to forget my nail scissors.

Laundry

Long trips mean you will need to wash clothes along the way. Some Airbnb hosts let you use the washing machine, but as there is usually no dryer, you'll have to wait while they dry naturally. Don't assume this is OK, check the profile when you book, and check with the host.

Image credit: Almunecar

The alternative is a coin laundry (*Laundromat* or *Launderette* in most countries) or a hand laundry (*Lavendaria*). Google Maps is quite unreliable in finding these, and will often direct you to a dry-cleaning place, where a small load of laundry can cost €30. I've taken to going into street-view and looking at the place, to see if it's the real thing. Local people generally don't use these, so you will find them in big cities and tourist centres, especially near bus or train stations.

Newspapers

I'm surely marking myself as a member of an obsolete generation, but I like to read an actual physical newspaper every day I can, so my first day in a new city often involves a search for a place that sells British ones. As a *Times* reader, naturally that's what I look for. You have to ask for the "London Times," or they'll sell you that colonial rag from New York. Apart from big cities in northern Europe, you'll be lucky to find it. As with books, the logical thing is to subscribe and read it on a screen, but for me that wouldn't be the same. In places, different papers are available. In Croatia, for example, they seem to only sell the *Daily Mail*, but I'm not that desperate. Kiosks near stations or ferries are your best bet.

Some countries have local or national newspapers in English, such as the Malta Times or the Prague Post. These may tell you about local festivals and events, and they're interesting in their own right.

Money

Don't change money in the UK, especially at airports. Your bank card will work in ATMs anywhere in Europe. Don't plan to pay for individual items using your bank card, as UK banks slap on a charge every time you do this. If you can, open a current account with a bank that doesn't.

I keep a permanent float of cash in Euros, as I travel a lot, but I change other currencies back as I leave, usually into Euros. Weighing down your bags with Polish Zlotys is just not worth what you lose on the exchange.

Medicines

If you need regular prescription medicines, take enough with you to cover the journey, as topping up abroad will be complicated. If you need over-the-counter medication while travelling, look for a pharmacy (*Farmacia*) – these are indicated by a lighted green cross throughout Europe. These are mostly strictly for medicines; you can't buy hair dryers or perfumes there.

Conclusion

I hope all these practical issues don't put you off foot-passenger travel. It's fun, if you approach any setbacks as part of the adventure and leave yourself plenty of time.

I would be happy to hear about your own journeys, and whether this book helped or got in the way. Do follow my Facebook page Foot Passenger Europe, and post on there any of your stories or pictures. I'll be posting pictures there of my next trip. Also let me know where I may have got things wrong.

I hope to issue a revised edition next year, and a PDF of that will be available free to purchasers of this book. Also see my website at footpassenger.org, where additional content may be added before that time. A PDF of this edition is available to paperback purchasers; just send me an e-mail.

Index

Printed in Great Britain
by Amazon

29213472R00064